Friends and Family

Mc
Graw
Hill
Education

Contents

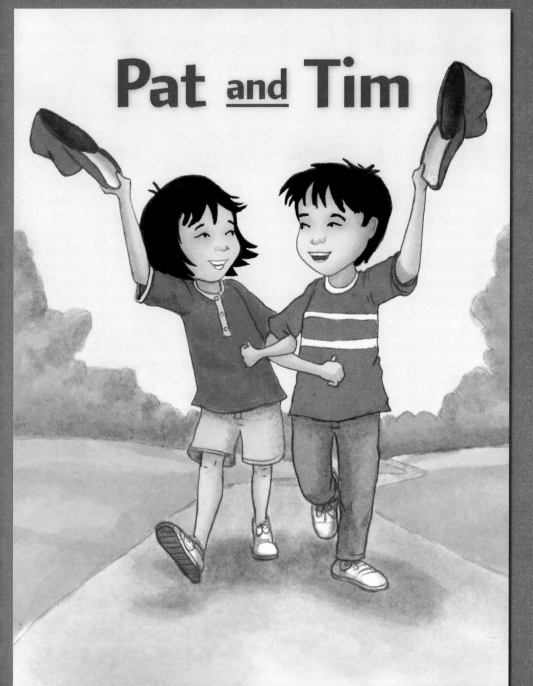

Pat and Tim

Pat and Tim are pals. Both Pat and Tim like caps. Pat and Tim put on caps. Both caps fit. In a bit, Pat and Tim will play.

Pat and Tim like t-ball. Pat and Tim play for the Cats. There are blue caps for the Cats. Pat and Tim win!

Where are Pat and Tim? Tim has a cap. Pat has a yellow cap. Why can caps help?

It is a big day for Pat and Tim. It is sad for the pals. Pat and Tim go in even if they are sad.

Pat has Miss P. in 2-P. Tim has
Miss B. in 2-B. Pat will miss Tim.
Tim will miss Pat!

Pals Help Pals

Kim has big bags in the van. Will and Zack can help Kim. Will has a big yellow bag. Zack has a big blue sack.

Zack, Kim, and Will are Rams. Will can kick it to Kim. Kim can kick it to Zack. Zack can kick it in.

Rams win!

Will is sick. Kim and Zack will help him. Will can sit back. Will can nap.

Kim, Will, and Zack help. Why?

Pals help pals!

Len and Gus

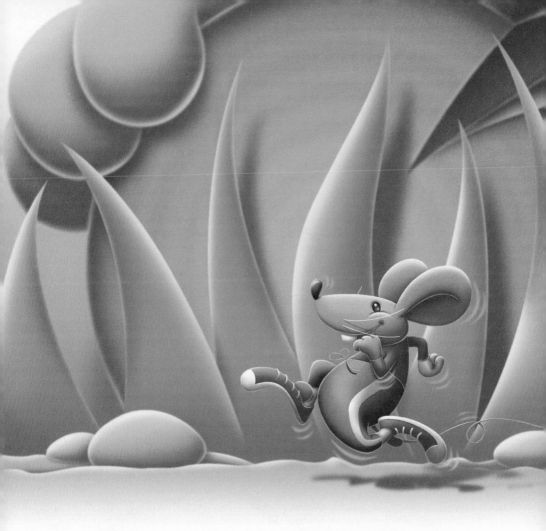

The sun was hot. Gus could see lots of green on his jog.

Gus ran. Gus had fun. But Gus did not see Len!

"I got you!" said Len. "I was up on a big log."

"Let go! I beg you!" said Gus.

"If you let go, I can help you."

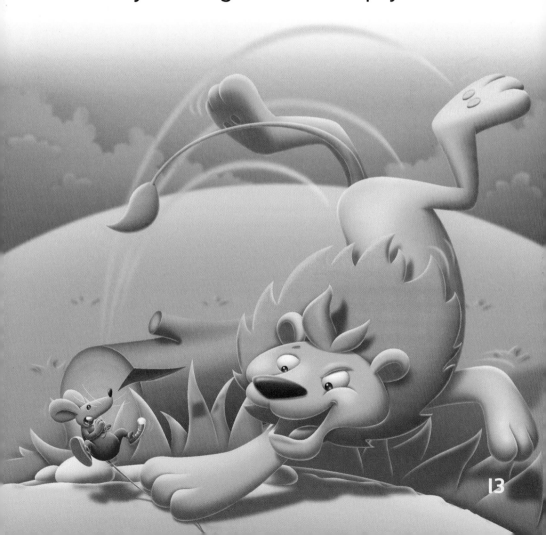

"How funny!" said Len. "You are not as big as a dog. How can one mouse help? But I will let go. Run, Gus, run!"

Gus ran.

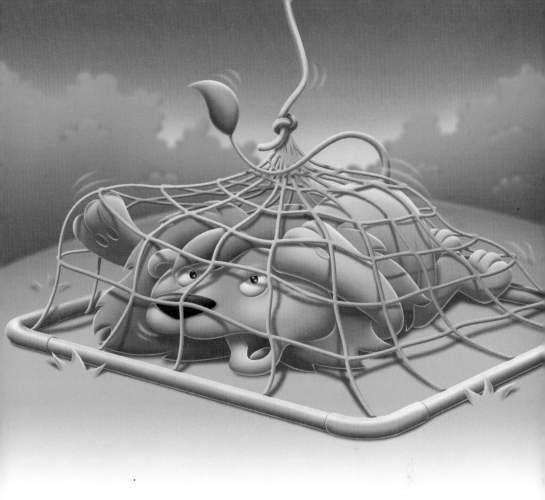

One day a big net fell on Len.
Len could not get up.

"HELP!" Len said. "Men set a net.
I am like a bug in a web!"

Gus was on a jog. "It sounds like Len!" Gus said. "I can help him. It is a job for a mouse!"

Gus ran to find Len.

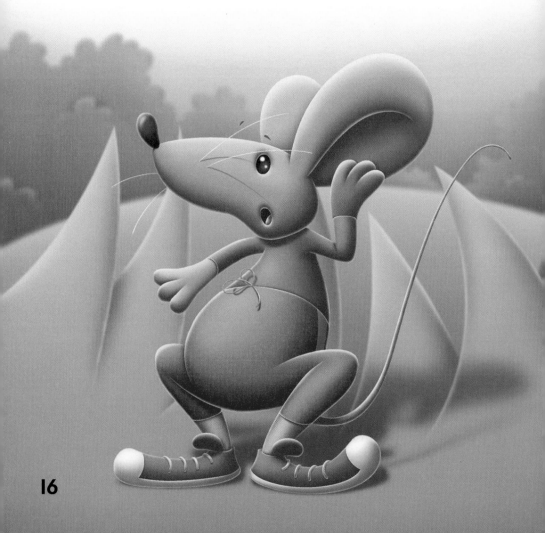

"I can help," said Gus. "I can cut the net."

"Get set and cut the net, or the men will get me!" said Len.

Gus got set. Gus bit the net. Gus bit and bit. The net was off! Len got up.

"You see," said Gus, "A *little* mouse can help a *big* lion."

Buses, Vans, Jets

Let us go see Nan. Let us get on a big bus. Big buses are fun!

Let us get on a jet. A jet hums.
A jet is quick. A jet is a lot of fun!

Let us hop up in a big van. Mom
packs boxes and Dad finds Sox the
cat. Pup sits in my lap. I pet little
Pup, and Mom pets Sox. Vans are fun!

Can you see us yet?

Spot
and
Fran

"Want to play?" asks Fran. Spot likes to play! Spot runs and gets twigs. He flips in the green grass.

"Stop! Stop!" yells Fran. But Spot can not stop.

Plop! Spot drops in the mud.
Spot has funny spots. Spot smells.
What can Fran do?

Fran has a plan. She grabs
a small tub and fills it up.

Spot hops in. He gets wet.
Fran rubs lots of suds on his spots.
But Spot can not sit still. He wants
to play.

Spot sees a boy and girl by the steps. Spot runs and trips on a pot. Plop! The pot spills on top of Spot.

"Where were you?" asks Fran.
"What did you do?"

Fran grins at Spot. "You are a mess, but I am glad you are here."

"Want to play?" asks Fran.

Why Not Grin?

If I am sad, I find Flip. Flip drops a stick on the grass. I toss it to him, and he grabs it.

I grin at him. Flip is fun, and I am not sad!

If I am mad, I find my small cats Flops and Mops. Flops licks my skin.

Mops is snug as she naps in my lap. I grin at Flops. I am not mad!

If I am glum, I find Duck. Duck
swims, spins, trips and dips.

I grin at Duck. He is funny, and I
am not glum!

Pets can help us grin. Pets are pals!

You Can
Bake a
Cake!

This year you and Dad can bake
a birthday cake for Mom. A cake is
fun to make. Dad has a cake mix.
Dad is glad he can help.

Ken O'Donoghue

Ask Dad to set the oven. Grab your cake pans. The cake mix will go into the pans. Set up the cake pans.

35

Get the cake box. Steps show how to make a cake. Mix the cake mix, water, and oil, too. Add an egg. Add another egg.

Cake

1. Heat oven.

2. Put in a bowl.

1 bag cake mix

$1\frac{1}{3}$ cups water

$\frac{1}{2}$ cup oil

2 eggs

3. Mix and bake.

Dad can mix it up. Fill up the cake pans. Set the cake pans in a hot oven. You and Dad can sit and wait.

Ken O'Donoghue

37

Let the cake bake. Move it to
a big plate. Frost the cake and dab
on red dots. Now you are done.
Mom is glad. Mom is going to take
this cake!

Ken O'Donoghue

Gabe Picks a Pet

Mom let Gabe take a pet. Gabe picked Jade.

"Can I get a cat, too?" Gabe asked Mom. "Can I take a cat? Or a black snake?"

"Get another pet?" Mom asked. "Not yet!"

Jade made a mess, and Gabe got it up. Jade was sick. Gabe had Mom take Jade to the vet.

Gabe made a bed for Jade. Jade got in it.

"Can I get a cat or a snake now?" asked Gabe. "I showed you I can take care of pets!"

Mom said, "Not yet, but we will see. I am glad you can take care of pets."

Mike's Big Bike

Mike rides his small bike.
As it moves, his legs hit the
handlebars. Mike likes his bike, but
he understands it is not the right
size. What will Mike do?

Mike tells Mom he has to get a big bike. Mom will help Mike pay for it. Mike will save up, too.

Mike gets to work. He rakes twigs.
He cuts grass.

Mike has a sale. He wipes the grill.
He fixes a man's kite. He works at
other jobs. Mike saves up.

Now Mike can get a fine new bike. Mike goes to Mr. Hide's sale. Mike sits on a green bike. He rides all of the bikes. Mike finds a bike he likes. It is the right size and the right price. Mike gets a red bike. It is a big bike!

Mike rides his red bike. Tim asks to ride it. Mike says, "You ride the big bike. I will ride the small bike. I can ride my big bike any time!" Mike and Tim smile.

A Site on Vine Lane

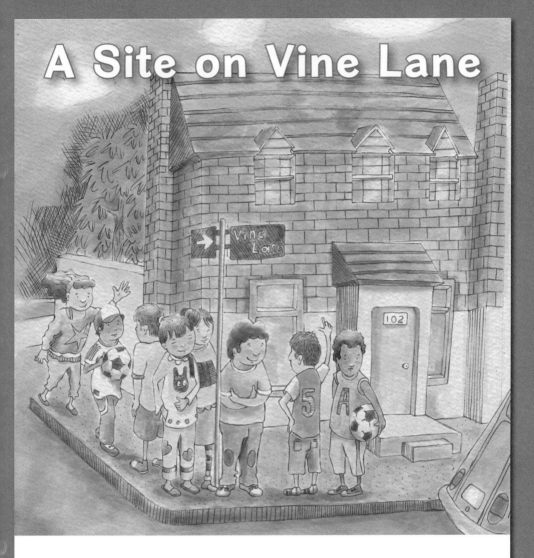

Kids on Vine Lane like playing ball. But where can they play? The kids on Vine Lane make a plan.

49

The kids find a mess on a big lot
on Vine Lane. The kids on Vine Lane
will work to fix it up.

Big kids cut the grass. Little kids pick up glass, cans, and rocks. The kids pile it all in a big bin. A big truck will take it to a new place.

The site is quite the right size. The kids on Vine Lane can kick, pass, and run! Big smiles fill the site!

52

Pat and Tim WORD COUNT: I2I

DECODABLE WORDS
Target Phonics Elements
Short *a**: and, cap, caps, Cats, has, Pat, pals, sad
Short *i**: bit, fit, in, is, it, miss, Tim, will, win

HIGH-FREQUENCY WORDS
ball, blue, both, even, for, help, put, there, why, yellow
Review: are, like, play, they
Story Word: day

Pals Help Pals WORD COUNT: 75

DECODABLE WORDS
Target Phonics Elements
Short *a**: Zack, Rams, can, back, pals, sack, bags, van, has, nap
Short *i**: big, him, is, it, kick, Kim, sick, sit, Will, win

HIGH-FREQUENCY WORDS
blue, help, why, yellow
Review: are, to, the

Len and Gus WORD COUNT: I90

DECODABLE WORDS
Target Phonics Elements
Short *e**: beg, fell, get, Len, let, men, net, set, web
Short *o**: dog, got, hot, job, jog, log, lots, not, off, on
Short *u**: but, cut, fun, Gus, run, sun, up

HIGH-FREQUENCY WORDS
could, find, funny, green, how, little, one, or, see, sounds
Review: are, for, go, help, like, me, of, said, the, to, was, you
Story Words: day, lion, mouse

Buses, Vans, Jets WORD COUNT: 77

DECODABLE WORDS
Target Phonics Elements
Short *e**: get, jet, let, pets, tells, yet
Short *o**: boxes, hop, lot, Mom, on, Sox
Short *u**: bus, fun, hums, Pup, up, us

HIGH-FREQUENCY WORDS
see, finds, little
Review: are, go, of, my

Spot and Fran WORD COUNT: I37

DECODABLE WORDS
Target Phonics Elements
Two-Letter Blends*; *r*-blends:
drops, Fran, frog, grabs, grass, grins;
***s*-blends:** smells, Spot, spots, steps, spills, still

***t*-blends:** trips, twigs; ***l*-blends:**
play, flips, plop, glad
HIGH-FREQUENCY WORDS
boy, by, girl, he, here, she, small, wants, were, what
Story Words: green

*Previously Taught

53

Why Not Grin?

DECODABLE WORDS

Target Phonics Elements
   Two-Letter Blends*; r-blends: drops, grabs, grin, grass; **s-blends:** skin, snug; **t-blends:** stick; **l-blends:** flip, flops, glum

HIGH-FREQUENCY WORDS

he, she, small
Review: are, find, funny, my, the, to, why

Week 4 **You Can Bake a Cake!**

WORD COUNT: 140

DECODABLE WORDS

Target Phonics Elements
   Short a*: add, an, ask, can, Dad, dab, grab, pans
   Long a: a_e*: bake, cake, make, plate, take

HIGH-FREQUENCY WORDS

another, done, into, move, now, show, too, water, year, your
Review: and, are, for, go, help, on, this, to, you
Story Words: birthday, oil, oven, wait

Gabe Picks a Pet

WORD COUNT: 105

DECODABLE WORDS

Target Phonics Elements
   Short a*: a, asked, can, cat. glad
   Long a*: Gabe, take, snake, made, Jade

HIGH-FREQUENCY WORDS

another, now, show, too
Review: for, of, or, see, said, the, to, was, you,
Story Words: care

Week 5 **Mike's Big Bike**

WORD COUNT: 176

DECODABLE WORDS

Target Phonics Elements
   Short i*: big, fixes, grill, his, hit, is, it, Tim, twigs, will
   Long i*: bike, bikes, fine, Hide's, kite, likes, Mike, ride, rides, size, smile, time, wipes

HIGH-FREQUENCY WORDS

all, any, goes, new, other, right, says, understands, work
Review: do, find, for, has, he, help, moves, my, now, of, small, the, to, too, what, you
Story Words: handlebars, pay, price

A Site on Vine Lane

WORD COUNT: 102

DECODABLE WORDS

Target Phonics Elements
   Short i*: big, bin, fill, fix, it. kids, pick, will
   Long i*: like, pile, quite, site, size, smiles, Vine

HIGH-FREQUENCY WORDS

all, new, right, work
Review: and, ball, is, find, little, playing, the, they, to, where

54

HIGH FREQUENCY WORDS

Grade K

a	animal	from	only	water
and	another	front	or	way
are	answer	full	other	were
can	any	fun	our	what
come	around	girl	out	who
do	away	give	over	why
does	be	gone	people	woman
for	been	good	picture	wonder
go	before	great	place	work
good	began	green	poor	would
has	better	grow	pretty	write
have	blue	guess	pull	year
he	boy	happy	push	young
help	brother	hard	put	your
here	brought	heard	question	
I	build	help	right	**Grade 2**
is	busy	her	round	all
like	buy	how	run	and
little	by	instead	school	another
look	call	into	should	any
me	carry	jump	small	are
my	caught	knew	so	ball
of	children	know	some	blue
play	climb	large	soon	both
said	color	laugh	start	boy
see	come	learn	sure	by
she	could	listen	surprise	could
the	day	live	their	do
they	does	love	then	done
this	done	make	there	even
to	door	many	they	find
too	down	money	thought	for
want	early	month	three	funny
was	eat	more	through	girl
we	eight	mother	today	go
what	enough	move	together	goes
where	every	near	tomorrow	green
who	eyes	new	too	has
with	fall	no	toward	he
you	father	none	two	help
	favorite	not	under	here
Grade 1	few	nothing	up	how
about	find	now	upon	into
above	flew	of	very	like
after	food	oh	use	little
again	found	old	walk	me
ago	four	once	want	move
all	friend	one	warm	my
				new
				now

number
of
on
one
or
other
play
put
right
said
says
see
she
show
small
some
sounds
the
there
they
this
to
too
understands
want
was
water
were
what
where
why
work
year
yellow
you
your

DECODING SKILLS TAUGHT TO DATE
short *a, i; -s, -es* (plural nouns); short *e, o, u; -s, -es* (inflectional endings); two-letter blends: *r*-blends, *s*-blends, *t*-blends, *l*-blends; closed Syllables; short *a,* long *a: a_e; -ed, -ing* (inflectional endings); short *i,* long *i: i_e;* possessives